George Washington's Rules *of* Civility *&* Decent Behavior

IN COMPANY AND CONVERSATION

George Washington

1

ISBN Numbers:
10 ISBN – Unassigned
13 ISBN – 978-1-312-25849-5

10 9 8 7 6 5 4 3 2 1

Formatting and Editing by: Silverwing Publishing
Introduction by: Mark W. Chidester
Artwork: Used under permission and/or as royalty free images.
Printed by: Lulu in the United States; subcontracted by Silverwing Publishing & Mark W. Chidester

George Washington's Rules for Civility and
Decent Behavior in Company and Conversation

INTRODUCTION

By age sixteen, Washington had copied out by hand, 110 *Rules of Civility & Decent Behavior in Company and Conversation*. They are based on a set of rules composed by French Jesuits in 1595. Presumably they were copied out as part of an exercise in penmanship assigned by young Washington's schoolmaster. The first English translation of the French rules appeared in 1640, most believe by Francis Hawkins the twelve-year-old son of a doctor.

Anyone that might read these rules today is likely to believe a number of them silly, and likely dismiss them as being 'outdated' and more 'appropriate to a time of quills and powdered wigs than a modern age,' but they reflect something that is increasingly difficult to find in today's high-tech world: focus.

"..and it may truly be said, that never did nature and fortune combine more perfectly to make a man great.."

– Thomas Jefferson,
about George Washington, 1814

The rules focus mostly upon other people rather than yourself, while most modern ideals are self-centric – that is they focus on yourself first, and others are merely an inconvenience that you must 'put up' with to survive.

Richard Brookhiser, *Founding Father: Rediscovering George Washington* (New York: Simon & Schuster Inc., 1996) pp. 130-131.

This collection of rules is ideal for today, in earnest, as they proclaim our respect for others (without needing to speak a word in most cases) and in turn give us a heightened self-esteem and the gift of self-respect.

Richard Brookhiser, in his book on Washington wrote that "all modern manners in the western world were originally aristocratic. *Courtesy* meant behavior appropriate to a court; *chivalry* comes from *chevalier* – a knight. Yet Washington was to dedicate himself to freeing America from a court's control. Could manners survive the operation?"

Just imagine if everyone in the nation practiced these rules. Imagine further being a beacon of hope to the world, that the entire world might embrace such a system, just how much greater a world we would have to leave to our children!

THE RULES:

1ST *Every Action done in Company, ought to be with Some Sign of Respect, to those that are Present.*
~ Modern: Treat everyone with respect.

2ND *When in Company, put not your Hands to any Part of the Body, not usually Discovered.*

3RD *Show Nothing to your Friend that may affright him.*
~ Modern: Be considerate of others. Do not embarrass others.

4TH *In the Presence of Others Sing not to yourself with a humming Noise, nor Drum with your*

Fingers or Feet.

5TH *If You Cough, Sneeze, Sigh, or Yawn, do it not Loud but Privately; and Speak not in your Yawning, but put Your handkerchief or Hand before your face and turn aside.*

6TH *Sleep not when others Speak, Sit not when others stand, Speak not when you Should hold your Peace, walk not on when others Stop.*

7TH *Put not off your Cloths in the presence of Others, nor go out your Chamber half Dressed.*

8 *TH* At Play and at Fire its Good
manners to Give Place to the
last Commer, and affect not to
Speak Louder than Ordinary.

9 *TH* Spit not in the Fire, nor Stoop
low before it neither Put your
Hands into the Flames to warm
them, nor Set your Feet upon
the Fire especially if there be
meat before it.

10 *TH* When you Sit down, Keep
your Feet firm and Even,
without putting one on the
other or Crossing them.

11TH *Shift not yourself in the Sight of others nor Gnaw your nails.*

12TH *Shake not the head, Feet, or Legs roll not the Eyes lift not one eyebrow higher than the other wry not the mouth, and bedew no mans face with your Spittle, by approaching too near him when you Speak.*

13TH *Kill no Vermin as Fleas, lice ticks &c in the Sight of Others, if you See any filth or thick Spittle put your foot Dexterously upon it if it be upon the Cloths of your Companions, Put it off privately, and if it be upon your own Cloths return Thanks to him who puts it off.*
~NOTE: "&c" here is et cetera, as in "and the others" or "and company"

14TH *Turn not your Back to others especially in Speaking, Jog not the Table or Desk on which Another reads or writes, lean not upon any one.*

15TH *Keep your Nails clean and Short, also your Hands and Teeth Clean yet without Showing any great Concern for them.*

16TH *Do not Puff up the Cheeks, Loll not out the tongue rub the Hands, or beard, thrust out the lips, or bite them or keep the Lips too open or too Close.*

~ Modern: Do not push out your cheeks, stick out your tongue, play with your face, stick out your lips, or keep your lips open wide (like snarling) or closed tight (like gritting teeth).

17TH *Be no Flatterer, neither Play with any that delights not to be Play'd Withal.*

18TH *Read no Letters, Books, or Papers in Company but when there is a Necessity for the doing of it you must ask leave: come not near the Books or Writings of Another so as to read them unless desired or give your opinion of them unasked also look not nigh when another is writing a Letter.*

19TH *Let your Countenance be pleasant but in Serious Matters Somewhat grave.*

20TH *The Gestures of the Body must be Suited to the discourse you are upon.*

21ST *Reproach none for the Infirmities of Nature, nor Delight to Put them that have in mind thereof.*

22ND *Show not yourself glad at the Misfortune of another though he were your enemy.*

23RD *When you see a Crime punished, you may be inwardly Pleased; but always show Pity to the Suffering Offender.*

24TH *Do not laugh too loud or too much at any Public Spectacle.*
~ Modern: Don't draw attention to yourself.

25TH *Superfluous Complements and all Affectation of Ceremony are to be avoided, yet where due they are not to be Neglected.*

26TH *In Pulling off your Hat to Persons of Distinction, as Noblemen, Justices, Churchmen &c make a Reverence, bowing more or less according to the Custom of the Better Bred, and Quality of the Person. Amongst your equals expect not always that they Should begin with you first, but to Pull off the Hat when there is no need is Affectation, in the Manner of Saluting and resaluting in words keep to the most usual Custom.*

27TH *Tis ill manners to bid one more eminent than yourself be covered as well as not to do it to whom it's due Likewise he that makes too much haste to Put on his hat does not well, yet he ought to Put it on at the first, or at most the Second time of being asked; now what is herein Spoken, of Qualification in behavior in Saluting, ought also to be observed in taking of Place, and Sitting down for ceremonies without Bounds is troublesome.*

28TH *If any one come to Speak to you while you are are Sitting Stand up though he be your Inferior, and when you Present Seats let it be to every one according to his Degree.*

29 *TH* When you meet with one of
Greater Quality than yourself,
Stop, and retire especially if it
be at a Door or any Straight
place to give way for him to
Pass.

30 *TH* In walking the highest Place
in most Countries Seems to be
on the right hand therefore
Place yourself on the left of him
whom you desire to Honor: but
if three walk together the
middest Place is the most
Honorable the wall is usually
given to the most worthy if two
walk together.

31ST *If any one far Surpasses
others, either in age, Estate, or
Merit yet would give Place to a
meaner than himself in his own
lodging or elsewhere the one
ought not to except it, So he on
the other part should not use
much earnestness nor offer it
above once or twice.*

32ND *To one that is your equal, or
not much inferior you are to
give the chief Place in your
Lodging and he to who 'is
offered ought at the first to
refuse it but at the Second to
accept though not without
acknowledging his own
unworthiness.*

33*RD* **They that are in Dignity or in office have in all places Precedency but whilst they are Young they ought to respect those that are their equals in Birth or other Qualities, though they have no Public charge.**

34*TH* *It is good Manners to prefer them to whom we Speak before ourselves especially if they be above us with whom in no Sort we ought to begin.*

~ Modern: When addressing a group, do not presume being the most knowledgeable on an issue; rather be willing to defer to others' opinions in their areas of expertise.

35*TH* *Let your Discourse with Men of Business be Short and Comprehensive.*

~ Modern: When you speak, be concise.

36TH *Artificers & Persons of low Degree ought not to use many ceremonies to Lords, or Others of high Degree but Respect and highly Honor them, and those of high Degree ought to treat them with affability & Courtesy, without Arrogance.*

37TH *In speaking to men of Quality do not lean nor Look them full in the Face, nor approach too near them at lest Keep a full Pace from them.*

38TH *In visiting the Sick, do not Presently play the Physician if you be not Knowing therein.*

39TH *In writing or Speaking, give to every Person his due Title According to his Degree & the Custom of the Place.*

40TH *Strive not with your Superiors in argument, but always Submit your Judgment to others with Modesty.*
~ Modern: Do not argue with your superior. Submit your ideas with humility.

41ST *Undertake not to Teach your equal in the art himself Professes; it Savours of arrogance.*

42ND *Let thy ceremonies in Courtesy be proper to the Dignity of his place with whom thou converses for it is absurd to act the same with a Clown and a Prince.*

43RD *Do not express Joy before
one sick or in pain for that
contrary Passion will
aggravate his Misery.*

44TH *When a man does all he can
though it Succeeds not well
blame not him that did it.*

~ *Modern: When a person does their
best and fails, do not criticize him.*

45TH *Being to advise or reprehend
any one, consider whether it
ought to be in public or in
Private; presently, or at Some
other time in what terms to do
it & in reproving Show no Sign
of Cholar but do it with all
Sweetness and Mildness.*

~ *Modern: When you must give advice
or criticism, consider the timing,
whether it should be given in public or
private, the manner and above all be
gentle.*

46TH *Take all Admonitions thankfully in what Time or Place Soever given but afterwards not being culpable take a Time & Place convenient to let him him know it that gave them.*
~ Modern: If you are corrected, take it without argument. If you were wrongly judged, correct it later.

47TH *Mock not nor Jest at any thing of Importance break [n]o Jest that are Sharp Biting and if you Deliver any thing witty and Pleasant abstain from Laughing thereat yourself.*
~ Modern: Do not make fun of anything important to others and do not laugh at your own jokes.

48TH *Wherein you reprove*
Another be unblameable
yourself; for example is more
prevalent than Precepts.

~ *Modern: If you criticize someone else*
of something, make sure you are not
guilty of it yourself. Actions speak
louder than words.

49TH *Use no Reproachful*
Language against any one
neither Curse nor Revile.

50TH *Be not hasty to believe*
flying Reports to the
Disparagement of any.

~ *Modern: Do not be quick to believe*
bad reports about others.

51ST *Wear not your Cloths, foul, ripped or Dusty but See they be Brushed once every day at least and take heed that you approach not to any Uncleaness.*

52ND *In your Apparel be Modest and endeavor to accommodate Nature, rather than to procure Admiration keep to the Fashion of your equals Such as are Civil and orderly with respect to Times and Places.*

53RD *Run not in the Streets, neither go too slowly nor with Mouth open go not Shaking your Arms kick not the earth with R feet, go not upon the Toes, nor in a Dancing fashion.*

54TH *Play not the Peacock, looking every where about you, to See if you be well Decked, if your Shoes fit well if your Stockings sit neatly, and Cloths handsomely.*

55TH *Eat not in the Streets, nor in the House, out of Season.*

56TH *Associate yourself with Men of good Quality if you Esteem your own Reputation; for 'is better to be alone than in bad Company.*
~ Modern: Associate with good people. It is better to be alone than in bad company.

57TH *In walking up and Down in a House, only with One in Company if he be Greater than yourself, at the first give him the Right hand and Stop not till he does and be not the first that turns, and when you do turn let it be with your face towards him, if he be a Man of Great Quality, walk not with him Cheek by Joul but Somewhat behind him; but yet in Such a Manner that he may easily Speak to you.*

58TH *Let your Conversation be without Malice or Envy, for 'is a Sign of a Tractable and Commendable Nature: And in all Causes of Passion admit Reason to Govern.*

~ Modern: Always allow reason to govern your actions.

59*TH* *Never express anything unbecoming, nor Act against the Rules Moral before your inferiors.*
~ Modern: Never break the rules in front of your subordinates.

60*TH* *Be not immodest in urging your Friends to Discover a Secret.*
~ Modern: Some things are better kept secret.

61*ST* *Utter not base and frivolous things amongst grave and Learned Men nor very Difficult Questions or Subjects, among the Ignorant or things hard to be believed, Stuff not your Discourse with Sentences amongst your Betters nor Equals.*

62ND Speak not of doleful Things
in a Time of Mirth or at the
Table; Speak not of Melancholy
Things as Death and Wounds,
and if others Mention them
Change if you can the Discourse
tell not your Dreams, but to
your intimate Friend.

63RD A Man ought not to value
himself of his Achievements, or
rare Qualities of wit; much less
of his riches Virtue or Kindred.
*~ Modern: A person should not overly
value their own accomplishments.*

64TH Break not a Jest where none
take pleasure in mirth Laugh
not aloud, nor at all without
Occasion, deride no mans
Misfortune, though there Seem
to be Some cause.

65TH *Speak not injurious Words neither in Jest nor Earnest Scoff at none although they give Occasion.*

66TH *Be not froward but friendly and Courteous; the first to Salute hear and answer & be not Pensive when it's a time to Converse.*

67TH *Detract not from others neither be excessive in Commanding.*
~ Modern: Do not detract from others nor be overbearing in giving orders.

68 *TH* Go not thither, where you know not, whether you Shall be Welcome or not. Give not Advice without being Asked & when desired do it briefly.

~ *Modern: Do not go where you are not wanted. Do not give unasked-for advice; and if asked, be brief.*

69 *TH* If two contend together take not the part of either unconstrained; and be not obstinate in your own Opinion, in Things indifferent be of the Major Side.

~ *Modern: If two people disagree, do not take one side or the other. Be flexible in your own opinions and when you don't care, take the majority opinion.*

70TH *Reprehend not the imperfections of others for that belongs to Parents Masters and Superiors.*
~ Modern: Do not correct others when it is not your place to do so.

71ST *Gaze not on the marks or blemishes of Others and ask not how they came. What you may Speak in Secret to your Friend deliver not before others.*

72ND *Speak not in an unknown Tongue in Company but in your own Language and that as those of Quality do and not as the Vulgar; Sublime matters treat Seriously.*

73RD **Think before you Speak**
pronounce not imperfectly nor
bring out your Words too
hastily but orderly & distinctly.

74TH **When Another Speaks be**
attentive your Self and disturb
not the Audience if any hesitate
in his Words help him not nor
Prompt him without desired,
Interrupt him not, nor Answer
him till his Speech be ended.

75TH **In the midst of Discourse ask**
not of what one treateth but if
you Perceive any Stop because
of your coming you may well
intreat him gently to Proceed: If
a Person of Quality comes in
while your Conversing it's
handsome to Repeat what was
said before.

76TH While you are talking, Point not with your Finger at him of Whom you Discourse nor Approach too near him to whom you talk especially to his face.

77TH Treat with men at fit Times about Business & Whisper not in the Company of Others.

78TH Make no Comparisons and if any of the Company be Commended for any brave act of Virtue, commend not another for the Same.

~ Modern: Don't compare yourselves amongst yourselves.

79TH **Be not apt to relate News if you know not the truth thereof. In Discoursing of things you Have heard Name not your Author always A Secret Discover not.**

~ Modern: Do not be quick to talk about something when you don't have all the facts.

80TH **Be not Tedious in Discourse or in reading unless you find the Company pleased therewith.**

81ST **Be not Curious to Know the Affairs of Others neither approach those that Speak in Private.**

~ Modern: Do not be curious about the affairs of others.

82ND *Undertake not what you cannot Perform but be Careful to keep your Promise.*
~ *Modern: Do not start what you cannot finish. Keep your promises.*

83RD *When you deliver a matter do it without Passion & with Discretion, however mean the Person be you do it too.*

84TH *When your Superiors talk to any Body hearken not neither Speak nor Laugh.*

85TH *In Company of these of Higher Quality than yourself Speak not til you are asked a Question then Stand upright put of your Hat & Answer in few words.*

86TH In Disputes, be not So
Desirous to Overcome as not to
give Liberty to each one to
deliver his Opinion and Submit
to the Judgment of the Major
Part especially if they are
Judges of the Dispute.

87TH Let thy carriage be such as
becomes a Man Grave Settled
and attentive to that which is
spoken. Contradict not at every
turn what others Say.

88TH Be not tedious in Discourse,
make not many Digressions,
nor repeat often the Same
manner of Discourse.

89TH Speak not Evil of the absent
for it is unjust.

~ Modern: Do not speak badly of those
who are not present.

90TH Being Set at meat Scratch not neither Spit Cough or blow your Nose except there's a Necessity for it.

91ST Make no Show of taking great Delight in your Victuals, Feed not with Greediness; cut your Bread with a Knife, lean not on the Table neither find fault with what you Eat.

92ND Take no Salt or cut Bread with your Knife Greasy.

93RD Entertaining any one at the table, it is decent to present him with meat; Undertake not to help others undesired by the Master.

94TH *If you Soak bread in the Sauce let it be no more than what you put in your Mouth at a time and blow not your broth at Table but Stay till Cools of it Self.*

95TH *Put not your meat to your Mouth with your Knife in your hand neither Spit forth the Stones of any fruit Pie upon a Dish nor Cast anything under the table.*

96TH *It's unbecoming to Stoop much to ones Meat Keep your Fingers clean & when foul wipe them on a Corner of your Table Napkin.*

97TH *Put not another bit into your mouth till the former be swallowed. Let not your morsels be too big for the jowls.*
~ Modern: Don't take so big a bite that you must chew with your mouth open.

98TH *Drink not nor talk with your mouth full; neither gaze about you while you are drinking.*

99TH *Drink not too leisurely nor yet too hastily. Before and after drinking, wipe your lips; breath not then or ever with too great a noise, for its uncivil.*

100TH Cleanse not your teeth with the table cloth napkin, fork, or knife; but if others do it, let it be done without a peep to them.

101ST Rinse not your mouth in the presence of others.

102ND It is out of use to call upon the company often to eat; nor need you drink to others every time you drink.

103RD In the company of your betters, be not longer in eating than they are; lay not your arm but only your hand upon the table.

104TH *It belongs to the chiefest in company to unfold his napkin and fall to meat first, but he ought then to begin in time & to dispatch with dexterity that the slowest may have time allowed him.*

105TH *Be not angry at the table whatever happens & if you have reason to be so, show it not; put on a cheerful countenance especially if there be strangers, for good humor makes one dish of meat a feast.*

106TH *Set not yourself at the upper of the table; but if it be your due or that the master of the house will have it so, contend not, least you should trouble the company.*

107TH *If others talk at the table, be attentive but talk not with meat in your mouth.*
~ Modern: Show interest in others conversation, but don't talk with your mouth full.

108TH *When you speak of God or his attributes, let it be seriously & with reverence. Honor & obey your natural parents although they be poor.*

109TH *Let your recreations be manful not sinful.*

110TH *Labor to keep alive in your breast that little spark of celestial fire called conscience.*
~ Modern: Don't allow yourself to become jaded, cynical or calloused.

FINIS

Note: Original spelling is unchanged.

www.ingramcontent.com/pod-product-compliance
Lightning Source LLC
Chambersburg PA
CBHW070345290526
45791CB00003B/1476